LIFE AFTER DEATH

LIFE AFTER DEATH

For Elizabeth — with your reflections on Reis + Shirley McLean, may you be prepared for now and the hereafter.

Allen

WHAT THE BIBLE SAYS

Allen F. Page

CONTEMPORARY
CHRISTIAN
CONCERNS
SERIES

JAMES M. EFIRD, EDITOR

ABINGDON PRESS
NASHVILLE

LIFE AFTER DEATH: WHAT THE BIBLE SAYS

This book is printed on acid-free paper.

Library of Congress Cataloging-in-Publication Data

PAGE, ALLEN F.
Life after death.
(Contemporary Christian concerns series)
Bibliography: p.
1. Future life—Biblical teaching. I. Efird, James M. II. Title.
III. Series.
BS680.F83P34   1987   236'.2   86-25850

ISBN 0-687-21733-4

Unless otherwise noted, all Scripture quotations from the Old
Testament, the New Testament, and the Apocrypha are from the
Revised Standard Version of the Bible, copyrighted 1946, 1952, © 1971,
1973 by the Division of Christian Education of the National Council of
the Churches of Christ in the U.S.A., and are used by permission.
Scripture quotations noted KJV are from the King James, or
Authorized, Version of the Bible.
Quotations from the Pseudepigrapha are from *The Apocrypha and
Pseudepigrapha*, vol. II, by R. H. Charles. Copyright 1913 by Oxford
University Press. Used by permission.

MANUFACTURED BY THE PARTHENON PRESS AT
NASHVILLE, TENNESSEE, UNITED STATES OF AMERICA

In Memoriam
Edwin Perry Page,
my brother

Gladys Blaylock Page
and
Hubert Leroy Page,
my parents

CONTENTS

*E*very person and every society have attempted to make some sense of life, but even more of the gnawing reality of physical death and its absolute certainty. Because of the uncertainty of life and the certainty of death, most people have developed euphemisms to designate that experience that no human being can avoid. One hears that this or that person now "sleeps with the ancestors," has "crossed the final frontier," has "fallen asleep," or is "no longer with us." These are only a few examples of the expressions created to combat the awe and dread that physical death strikes in the hearts of all people.

In this series, which attempts to examine what the Bible says about human concerns, it is especially appropriate that a volume be included discussing the biblical view of life after death. To examine this topic is not an easy task because so many people confuse and conflate the biblical teachings about this subject with other ideas about Jesus' return, resurrection, the consummation of the kingdom, and the final conclusion of history. Dr. Allen F. Page, Professor of Religion at Meredith College in Raleigh, North Carolina, has done an admirable job of presenting the biblical teachings about life after death in this volume. He has shown how the ideas about this topic developed in the history of Israelite religion, how these views were broadened during the intertestamental period (around 150 B.C.–A.D. 50), and how these ideas were used and modified by Jesus and the New Testament writers.

What one finds is a progression of thought in this area that is firmly based on the nature of God and God's relationship with those who chose to participate in the covenant community. It was only a matter of time before these principles led to the great affirmation of the New Testament writers that the fear of physical death had been removed for those in the proper relationship with God. This relationship transcends the frailty of human existence because God is the Lord of life. Their affirmation is well stated in Paul's great statement: "Death is swallowed up in victory" (I Cor. 15:54). The victory, of course, is God's, demonstrated to the world in concrete terms through the resurrection of Jesus of Nazareth.

Dr. Page has done a fine job of leading the reader

into a better understanding of this intricate and intriguing topic. It is his hope and mine that this book and series will serve to assist people in correctly understanding important biblical topics.

JAMES M. EFIRD

*T*his book is about the views of life after death which are expressed in biblical literature. The ideas contained in this work are those with which I have worked for a long time. My concern with these ideas has been both an intellectual journey and an intense personal struggle in response to the deaths of people who have made a significant impact on my life.

The formulation of these ideas began during my work at Union Theological Seminary in New York. (My thesis title was "Paul's Understanding of the Resurrection: An Exegesis of I Corinthians 15.") I am indebted to Dr. John Knox for his guidance, as my thesis advisor, and for his continuing friendship. He has been a mentor in many ways.

The most immediate stimulus for this book was an invitation from Dr. James M. Efird to write a short volume on this topic in the series *Contemporary Christian Concerns*. I was more than pleased to accept this invitation because it provided the opportunity to work with a longtime acquaintance whose friendship I have valued for more than twenty years. His kind encouragement and criticism have helped to shape this project.

Since I began writing in the summer of 1985, several groups of people have been willing audiences and critics of my ideas. I express my appreciation to members of First Baptist Church in Raleigh, North Carolina, who were participants in a retreat at Ridgecrest, North Carolina, in October 1985. Also, the congregation of Pullen Memorial Baptist Church in Raleigh, North Carolina, provided encouragement through their questions and affirmation following a lecture in January 1986.

During the fall semester of 1985 and the spring semester of 1986, I taught a seminar entitled "Biblical Views of Life After Death." The continuing study and dialogue with students who were in these seminars at Meredith College have been beneficial in the shaping and refining of my ideas. To these students, I convey my deep appreciation for their contributions to the shaping of this work.

Verbal expression is the necessary vehicle for communicating ideas. I am grateful to Dr. Linda Barlow, a friend and colleague at Meredith, who has willingly assisted in reading my manuscript with a critical eye to make the verbal expression a more effective medium.

Finally, I express my deepest appreciation to Barbara, my wife, who has worked with dedication to transfer my often scribbled handwriting into the memory of our word processor. In addition, she has offered by word and presence her encouragement and support, both of which have made the completion of this manuscript an easier task.

What is going to happen to me when I die? That is one of the most fundamental questions that humankind has struggled with throughout the whole of recorded history.

While intellectual historians have attempted to talk objectively about trends and schools of thought about life after death, the fundamental question continues to be an emotional concern, claiming the attention of and creating anxiety for most individuals. My earliest personal reflection on this question was on the occasion of the death of a neighbor when I was three and one-half years old. On the morning of Mr. Green's funeral, I sat in the kitchen watching my mother cook. I remember asking a series of questions: "What is it like to die? Will Mr. Green be at his funeral? How will he get to the cemetery? . . . "

My mother explained, in what I remember as very patient tones, that being dead was something like being asleep. Mr. Green's body would be at the funeral, but he would not be able to see or hear because his soul had gone to heaven as soon as he died. Mr. Green would be carried to the cemetery by his friends. As she made these comments, my mind envisioned four men, holding his hands and feet in a very awkward procession. "No," my mother said, "they will put him in a box." Again my imagination created its own scene. I could see an image of a very long cardboard box that buckled in the middle just as they were crossing the highway from the church to the cemetery and the men scurrying to keep Mr. Green from falling out onto the pavement. All this imagining was more reminiscent of the "Keystone Kops" escapades than of the tone of seriousness I thought appropriate to a funeral. I was relieved that afternoon at the funeral to discover that a more substantial box was being used and that I could relax. The sense of peace was to last for only a moment because soon I was consumed by a more lasting and pragmatic anxiety: How would Mr. Green avoid getting dirt in his eyes when they filled in the grave?

When my older daughter, Ellen, was five years old, we visited her grandparents for Thanksgiving. In a discussion after supper one evening, she asked her grandmother, "Where is your mother?" Her grandmother responded that her mother had died before Ellen was born. Ellen's grandmother then went on to say that Ellen reminded her of her own mother and that she believed that part of Ellen's great-grand-mother would always be a part of Ellen. When we returned home after Thanksgiving, our neighbor in the apartment complex had given birth to a daughter. When mother and baby came home from the hospital, Ellen went over to see them. That night, as I was helping Ellen get ready for bed, she said, "People die, don't they?" I responded, "Yes, they do." I then reminded her of her conversation with her grandmother. She thought a moment and said, "But people are born, too, aren't they?" Reassuringly I said, "Yes," and reminded her of her visit with the new little baby. Her next comment was more a statement than a question as she said, "That means there will always be people, doesn't it?"

My personal experiences have initiated my reflections on life after death. No single event in my life has been more theologically troublesome for me than the death of a friend who was killed when a tractor overturned. I was fourteen years old then, and I remember asking, "Why?" The pain I felt also caused me to question the glibly stated phrase, "He's better off," that was offered by others to reassure me. Better off? At sixteen years old? My mind was filled with questions. Largely, these questions were suppressed. This curiosity was, nevertheless, the beginning of an ongoing concern with the question of life after death. Without a doubt, the deaths of the infant children of two of my brothers further stimulated my curiosity about this issue.

These wrestlings and the resultant reflections

served as a stimulus for the selection of the topic of my master's thesis, "Paul's Understanding of the Resurrection: An Exegesis of I Corinthians 15." Ultimately, it was the death of my brother Ed of cancer at age thirty that caused me to come to some theological and inward peace about death. Though wrenched by his loss, I found solace in the twin affirmations of biblical truth: "You are dust, and to dust you shall return" (Gen. 3:19) and "Not even death can separate us from the love of God" (see Rom. 8:35-39).

Conversations with others revealed that I am not alone in the struggle to make sense of the question of life after death. Often these quests are not very focused, but sometimes they are. For example, in a recent conversation with a friend, following the death of his father, my friend asked with both hope and fear, "Can my father look down and know what I am doing and thinking?"

It is for people who are experiencing such reflections about death that this book is written and for whom it is intended. I write with the conviction that, for those of us who claim our identity in relation to the Christian tradition, it is important to know what the Bible says about the question of life after death. We profit by knowing the theological truths that the Bible affirms as well as the cultural contexts that have shaped the affirmation. It is my hope that the attempt to clarify these issues will stimulate and foster continuing theological reflection.

In dealing with the question of life after death,

there are many areas of thought that impinge upon one's reflection. There is an obvious overlap with broader questions dealing with the end of the age and the consummation of the kingdom of God. These questions often are not separated from the more specific teachings about life after death. Although these questions are related, in this work there will be a conscious effort to focus on life after death.

When speaking of the biblical perspective, the word *views* rather than *view* is used intentionally, because not all the writers of the biblical tradition comprehend life after death from the same perspective. The breadth and variety of the biblical tradition are a part of its richness. In the first three chapters that follow, we shall explore this breadth and variety of biblical expressions. In the final chapter, we shall make some observations and draw some conclusions that focus on a biblical understanding of life after death.

CHAPTER I

Basic Old Testament
Views of Death

*I*n the beginning God created the heavens and the earth. As God designed and implemented creation, "Behold, it was very good!" (Gen. 1:3).

As the biblical story reflects on this creation, humanity is the crown and glory of all that is. Humankind is unique. As the psalmist says, "Thou hast made him little less than God, and dost crown him with glory and honor" (Ps. 8:5).

Genesis affirms that God created humankind (male and female) in God's own image (see Gen. 1:26). Passages such as this are, however, balanced by references to the transient nature of human existence, which suggests that it shares the temporary character of all biological creatures. "You are dust, and to dust you shall return" (Gen. 3:19). In Genesis 18:27, Abraham says, "Behold I have taken upon myself to speak to the Lord, I who am but dust and ashes." Humanity's transient character is further expressed in the words of Isaiah 40:6-7:

> All flesh is grass,
>   and all its beauty is like the flower of the field.
> The grass withers, the flower fades,
>   when the breath of the Lord blows upon it;
>   surely the people is grass.

Collectively the biblical narrative presents a tension between the God-related and eternal dimension of human life and the fleeting, transient, perishable dimension.

Attempting to discuss the patterns of the development of biblical material with reference to the nature of humankind and of its eternal character is not without problems. A common approach has been to view all of biblical tradition as making the same affirmation. Thus, if one book speaks of heaven and hell with rewards and punishments in the hereafter, that concept must also necessarily, it is thought, be seen throughout biblical literature from Genesis to Revelation.

The inadequacy of this view is clear to all who take seriously the historical study of the Bible. The problem of understanding the development of the biblical teachings is not so simple as working through the biblical tradition from Genesis forward. The books of the Bible are not arranged chronologically, nor are the traditions included in each book merely the historical reflections of the final author or editor. Most books reflect various levels of understanding appropriate to the transmission of tradition through oral, as well as written, stages. For example, the Pentateuch expresses not only the memories passed on orally from the times of the patriarchs and the Exodus, but also the cultural and theological presuppositions and concepts of the historical periods of the authors and editors from the tenth century until the sixth century B.C.

In making observations about the development of ideas in the biblical tradition, one may much more easily speak of a profile and patterns that emerge than about the evolution of a specific chronology of exact events or ideas. This assertion about the evolution of biblical literature needs to be kept in mind as we proceed.

The emphasis in the Old Testament is on God as God of the living; the Omnipotent One, who gives life and takes it away. In the first account of creation (there are two different accounts of creation—Gen. 1:1–2:3 and 2:4–3:24), God formed humanity as the culmination of all creation at the beginning of the world.

> So God created man in his own image, in the image of God he created him; male and female he created them. Genesis 1:27

In the second account of creation,

> The Lord God formed man of dust from the ground, and breathed into his nostrils the breath of life; and man became a living being. Genesis 2:7

Humanity shares with the whole animal kingdom the gift of the breath of life (Gen. 6:17). Thus the "breath of life" is not that which gives humankind its distinctiveness as children of God. Rather the account describes humankind as being animated in much the way we perceive that a spirited horse is very much alive. This life, itself, is a gift from God for humans and beasts alike.

The description of people becoming "living beings" reveals more about humans as special creatures of God than does the phrase "breath of life." The thrust of the description is comparable to the description of humanity's being created in God's own image in the first account (see Gen. 1:26). As living beings humans have an unparalleled place in God's scheme of creation.

To say that "man became a living being" is for the biblical writer a forthright statement. In Hebrew, the term translated as "living being" is *nephesh,* meaning "life principle," "life force," or "individual expression of life." The word is sometimes used as an equivalent of "breath" or "throat." In Psalm 69:1 the writer pleads for help: "Save me, O God! For the waters have come up to my neck [nephesh]." Sometimes nephesh has extremely animated and passionate implications, as in Genesis 34:3, in which the desire of Shechem the Hivite for Dinah is described by the phrase "and his soul [nephesh] was drawn to Dinah."

Nephesh is usually used to describe a person who is alive. It is not some detachable aspect of humanity that has an independent existence, as is the case with the Greek concept of the "soul." To some Greek thinkers, the "soul" was thought to have an independent existence both before and after its incarnation in a physical body. Indeed it is unfortunate that the word *nephesh* came to be translated as "soul" in many popular English translations. Such a translation imposes on the Old Testament passages concepts from later thinking and from different cultures. It is important to remember that, for the ancient Hebrew, nephesh was an aspect of life itself. In the same way, a body is never seen as having existence independently of the nephesh, except when it is a corpse. In Hebrew thought, there is no dichotomy of components that make up the human person. Nephesh, body, spirit, mind, and many other realities described in the Old Testament are aspects of humanity. While it is possible to isolate these individual aspects as characteristics of a living person, they can never be appropriately viewed in isolation. Each person is always a living being (nephesh) and each living being is special to God.

At life's end, a person is no longer described as a living being (nephesh). At the end of one's days, death comes to each human being as to all other living things. With overwhelming finality, the fate of humanity is described again and again in simple terms: "And he died" (Gen. 5:5; 5:8; 5:14; 5:17; 5:25; 5:31; and others).

What happens when one dies? The psalmist describes vividly that finality facing all:

Truly no man can ransom himself,
  or give to God the price of his life,
for the ransom of his life is costly,
  and can never suffice,
that he could continue to live on for ever,
  and never see the Pit.
Yea, he shall see that even the wise die,
  the fool and the stupid alike must perish
  and leave their wealth to others.
Their graves are their homes for ever,
  their dwelling places to all generations,
  though they named lands their own.
Man cannot abide in his pomp,
  he is like the beasts that perish.

Psalm 49:7-12

Repeatedly, Old Testament figures are described by reference to family or ancestors: "and he slept with his fathers" (see Gen. 47:30 and I Kings 2:10) or "he was gathered to his people" (see Gen. 5:29; 25:8; 49:33; and Deut. 32:50) or "gathered to their fathers" (Judg. 2:10). These descriptions suggest an emphasis on a common familial burial site, such as described in Genesis 23, in which Abraham purchased the field in Machpelah as the burial place for Sarah. In this field was a cave that was the burial place not only for Sarah, but also for Abraham, Isaac, Rebekah, and Leah (Gen. 49:29-30). On his deathbed, Jacob charged his sons to "bury me with my fathers" in this same cave (Gen. 49:29). He was taken back to the cave and buried there. Family member after family member was buried in a bench-like grave in such cave tombs. Bones were likely gathered to a common area to make room for those who died later. Thus the dead in ancient Israel were literally gathered to their people. This tradition was a common practice that evolved to such an extent that Barzilli longed to lie down "near the grave of [his] father and mother" (II Sam. 19:37). Not to be allowed to be buried with one's father came to be regarded as dishonor. In Jeremiah 26:23, Uriah was killed and buried with the common people in contrast to being buried with his own family.

In time, the idea of being gathered to one's people was shaped into the concept of a dwelling place for the dead. Although it is not possible to trace the imaginative development of this idea, the concept of *Sheol* emerged quite early in Hebrew thinking. Even the meaning of the word is unclear. Some scholars have traced the etymology of the word so as to focus on Sheol as a "hollowed" place, perhaps as an extension of the grave as a place that has been hollowed out.

The term *Sheol* is, however, derived from the Hebrew word meaning "to ask" or "to inquire." Some scholars suggest that the term is indicative of an early view that Sheol was a realm from which oracles were sought from the dead. Second Samuel 28 is sometimes cited as an example of this activity. In this passage, a disturbed Saul has the medium of Endor call up the spirit of Samuel from the realm of Sheol. This practice was, however, officially taboo among the ancient Israelites (see Exod. 22:18; Lev. 2:27; and II Kings 23:24) and thus does not seem to suggest a norm for explaining Israel's understanding. A more helpful suggestion is that the term *Sheol* is itself an explanation of the question, "What happens after death?" It suggests that what happens beyond death is known only to God. As the Law says, "The secret things belong to the Lord our God; but the things that are revealed belong to us" (Deut. 29:29). If this meaning can be accepted, the Hebrew concept of Sheol is the most honest expression imaginable that we indeed do not know what happens at death.

Whatever its derivation, however, Sheol is the realm of the dead. There are intimations that at death a shadowy image of the dead continued in some barren, quasi-human form. The spirit that makes a human being is withdrawn. Man literally expires and, like other animals, returns to dust.

The traditional view of Sheol is that it is a place to which all the dead go. It cannot be described in terms of life after death. As a shadowy realm, it reflects an honest expression of the uncertainty of what happens beyond death. Yet as a realm of darkness and desolation, Sheol is an affirmation of the finality of death.

Several selected passages from the Old Testament convey images of what Sheol is like.

Your pomp is brought down to Sheol,
   the sound of your harps;
maggots are the bed beneath you,
   and worms are your covering.

                     Isaiah 14:11

Remember that my life is a breath;
   my eye will never again see good.

The eye of him who sees me will
    behold me no more;
  while thy eyes are upon me, I shall be gone.
As the cloud fades and vanishes,
  so he who goes down to Sheol does
    not come up.

Job 7:8-9

For in death there is no remembrance of thee;
  in Sheol who can give thee praise?

Psalm 6:5

What profit is there in my death,
  if I go down to the Pit?
Will the dust praise thee?
  Will it tell of thy faithfulness?

Psalm 30:9

In its basic affirmation, the concept of Sheol is negative primarily in terms of its finality. There is no end to its silence and darkness. Accordingly, Job's plea is for a moment's peace before his descent into Sheol:

Why didst thou bring me forth from the womb?
Would that I had died before any eye had seen me,
and were as though I had not been,
  carried from the womb to the grave.
Are not the days of my life few?
  Let me alone, that I may find a little comfort
before I go whence I shall not return,
  to the land of gloom and deep darkness,
the land of gloom and chaos,
  where light is as darkness.

Job 10:18-22

This finality is expressed in terms that suggest that at death the dead have no further relationship with

God. This idea seems also to be implied in the question of Psalm 88:11-12:

Is thy steadfast love declared in the grave,
or thy faithfulness in Abaddon?
Are thy wonders known in the darkness,
or thy saving help in the land of forgetfulness?

The psalmist further notes,

The dead do not praise the Lord,
nor do any that go down into silence.

Psalm 115:17.

The same idea is expressed in Isaiah 38:18:

For Sheol cannot thank thee,
death cannot praise thee;
those who go down to the pit cannot hope
for thy faithfulness.

Sheol is usually described spatially as being "down." This concept reflects the view of the three-storied universe, which is typical of the Old Testament. Earth is between the heavenly abode of God, who sits in a royal court, and an abyss out of which spring mountains that support the earth.

The dead are described as returning to the earth. When "Pharaoh's chariots and his host" are cast into the sea (Exod. 15:4), we are told that "the earth swallowed them" (Exod. 15:12). The Genesis narrative depicts the ground as swallowing up the blood (i.e., life) of Abel when he is murdered by Cain. "You are cursed from the ground, which has opened its mouth to receive your brother's blood from your hand" (Gen. 4:11). Again, in Numbers 16:31-35, the ground swallows up victims in a trauma of destruction:

> And as he [Moses] finished speaking all these words, the ground under them split asunder: and the earth opened its mouth and swallowed them up, with their households and all the men that belonged to Korah and all their goods. So they and all that belonged to them went down alive into Sheol; and the earth closed over them and they perished from the midst of the assembly. And all Israel that were round about them fled at their cry; for they said, "Lest the earth swallow us up!" And fire came forth from the Lord, and consumed the two hundred and fifty men offering the incense.

While this episode has overtones of retribution, it affirms that the final resting place of the dead is deep within the earth. This belief is consistent with other passages that speak of Sheol as a pit (Job 33:18; Ps. 16:10; 30:10; 38:1; 88:4; Isa. 14:9; 38:17; 51:14; Jon. 2:6). A few Old Testament passages speak of Sheol as being the deepest level of earth. In speaking of Egypt, the prophet Ezekiel says, "For they are all given over to death, to the nether world among mortal men, with those who go down to the Pit" (Ezek. 31:14).

The relative unimportance of the dead is clearly a characteristic belief of the people of ancient Israel. The Old Testament places primary emphasis on the

God of the living. It is true, however, that the God of the living is regarded as having control over all, and thus is considered to have control even over the realm of the dead. This concept is the affirmation of the book of Amos, in saying that none can escape the judgment of God.

> Though they dig into Sheol,
>   from there shall my hand take them;
> though they climb up to heaven,
>   from there I will bring them down.
>
> Amos 9:2

Similarly, the psalmist says,

> If I ascend to heaven, thou art there!
> If I make my bed in Sheol, thou art there!
>
> Psalm 139:8

It was noted above that a person retains a quasi-human dimension at death, even though the spirit which makes that person a living being is withdrawn. This belief led the Hebrews to make efforts to communicate with the dead, apparently fostered by neighboring cultures for which communication with the dead was common. The clearest example of the wish to speak to the dead is seen in Saul's attempt to communicate with Samuel when it appeared that the Philistine menace would be more than Saul had bargained for (I Sam. 28). Saul himself had "cut off the mediums and the wizards from the land" (v. 9) in conjunction with the taboo of ancient Israel that one should not have contact (physical or otherwise) with the dead. Saul thus disguised himself when he approached the medium at Endor and asked that she "bring up Samuel" for him (v. 11). The returning response is striking when he says, "Why have you disturbed me by bringing me up?" (v. 15). That there is an entity capable of being recalled is unusual in the literature of the Old Testament. The persistent attempt to repress the practice of consulting mediums and wizards (as seen in Lev. 20:27 and II Kings 23:24) suggests that this view of a person's being brought back for consultation is not typical of the view of ancient Israel. It is, in fact, contrary to the more typical affirmation of the finality of death that we see in the Old Testament.

The finality of death is a pervasive affirmation in the Old Testament. There is no immortality in terms of what later came to be expressed as a belief in life after death with rewards and punishments. Rewards are thought of as being enjoyed in this life. The primary criterion for rewards is obedience to or faith in God; for example, Abraham had faith in God and thus was rewarded (Gen. 15:6).

When given the Ten Commandments, the people were told that they would be rewarded for obedience to those commandments. In Exodus 20:12, the reward for honoring father and mother is that "your days may be long" upon the earth. Likewise, in the early chapters of Genesis, those who are the God-fearing forerunners of the patriarchs are described as living long and full lives. The most extreme example is Methuselah, who is said to have lived nine hundred and sixty-nine years (Gen. 5:27). Consistently in the Old Testament there is a view of cause and effect: obey God and prosper; disobey and be judged. This view is often referred to as the deuteronomic view of history. Prosperity is seen primarily in terms of longevity of life. The gifts of children and property established or enhanced a reputation that lived on beyond the death of the individual. Punishment is seen as a denial of these rewards.

The immortal gift of reputation is not an extension of one's life, but an extension of one's influence. Since one is generally remembered most tenaciously by one's children, children not only assure biological continuity, but they also are the guarantors of the memory of the forebears. For this reason, in ancient Israel it was regarded as a tragedy to die childless. The force of this tradition (among other factors) lies behind the use of concubines to bear children, as seen in the examples of Sarah, Rachel, and Leah in the Genesis narrative. The tradition is expressed with even greater power in the custom of levirate marriage, whereby if a man died childless it was the responsibility of the male next-of-kin to father a child by the widow in the name of the deceased. This view is expressed most clearly in Deuteronomy 25:5-6:

> If brothers dwell together, and one of them dies and has no son, the wife of the dead shall not be married outside the family to a stranger; her husband's brother shall go in to her, and take her as his wife,

and perform the duty of a husband's brother to her. And the first son whom she bears shall succeed to the name of his brother who is dead, that his name may not be blotted out of Israel.

Although memory and the act of remembering are, in the Old Testament, primarily focused on the acts of God on behalf of his people, remembering one's forebears was also significant. Honoring the memory of one's forebears serves as a model for living in the present. The people of Israel are praised or scorned according to whether they "take care to walk in the way of the Lord as their fathers did" (Judg. 2:22). Josiah, for example, is praised because he "walked in all the way of David his father, and he did not turn aside to the right hand or to the left" (II Kings 22:2). The remembrance of forebears has an even greater significance for the community than for the individual in ancient Israel. It is remarkable that two of the most important affirmations of faith focus on the forebears of Israel. In the book of Joshua there is the affirmation, "I took your father Abraham from beyond the River and led him through all the land of Canaan, and made his offspring many" (24:3). The account goes on to acclaim what God has done for and through other forebears. In Deuteronomy 26:5, the appropriate response to God that each Israelite makes upon entering the land of Canaan is: "A wandering Aramean was my father; and he went down into Egypt and sojourned there, few in number; and there he became a nation, great, mighty, and populous." These passages reflect an awareness that is abundantly clear in the Old Testament, namely, that there is a much greater stress on corporate consciousness than is the case in our more individualistic Western culture. In the Old Testament, the individual has primary significance only in the context of community. Even God's promises to Abraham have their focus in the people who are his descendants and in the land they will possess. The survival of the family, the clan, and the nation is a significant point of focus.

It is important to note that the deuteronomic view of rewards and punishments is applied not only to the individual, but also to the community. In Exodus 18 the promise made in the invitation to establish a covenant with God is that if the people will keep his commandments, God will make them a kingdom of priests. This promise is a communal one. In Judges the cycle of rewards and punishments, which is reported in great detail, affects the whole community of the tribal confederation. Their disobedience by turning to the gods of the Canaanites is punished by oppression at the hands of neighboring peoples. When the Israelites repent, God sends a judge who delivers them from their oppression.

As the Old Testament story develops, it is the survival of the house of David that becomes crucial. The prophets focus their attention on the restoration of the fallen nation, for the corporate whole is greater than any individual.

From the time that the history of Israel moved into the period of the monarchy, her corporate identity was allied with that of the nation. The hopes for her future came to be inseparable from the fate of the nation. The covenant with David ties this corporate hope to the lineage of David; the hope of Israel is that the Davidic line will last forever: "And your house and your kingdom shall be made sure for ever before me; your throne shall be established for ever" (II Sam. 7:16). When the kingdom became divided after the reign of Solomon, with Israel being the northern kingdom and Judah the southern kingdom, the continuity of corporate hope remained tied to the house of David in the south, especially after the destruction of the northern kingdom at the hands of Assyria in 721 B.C. Judah became the heir and preserver of all the literary and theological traditions; the final editing of these traditions assumes and affirms the continuity of national hope through the house of David. The prophet Amos proclaims:

> Fallen, no more to rise,
>   is the virgin Israel;
> forsaken on her land,
>   with none to raise her up.
>
> Amos 5:2

A later editor of the book of Amos has transferred its hope from the extinct northern kingdom of Israel to the southern kingdom, which by this time had fallen to the Babylonians.

> In that day I will raise up
>   the booth of David that is fallen
> and repair its breaches,

and raise up its ruins,
and rebuild it as in the days of old.

Amos 9:11

In periods of national crisis, the prophetic affirmations of hope were often pleas for a return to the
"good old days." In the prophetic oracles of Isaiah,
there is the hope for an ideal ruler who will be like
David.

For to us a child is born,
to us a son is given;
and the government will be upon his shoulder,
and his name will be called
"Wonderful Counselor, Mighty God,
Everlasting Father, Prince of Peace."
Of the increase of his government and of peace
there will be no end,
upon the throne of David, and over his kingdom,
to establish it, and to uphold it
with justice and with righteousness
from this time forth and for evermore.

Isaiah 9:6-7

Even though there is strong hope for a Davidic
leader, an equally important aspect of the hope for
the return of the "good old days" is the expectation of
restoring the ideal state of creation and of Israel
itself. In Isaiah 11 the Davidic ruler will be
instrumental in the return to the state of tranquility
that was characteristic of creation.

There shall come forth a shoot from the stump of
Jesse,

and a branch shall grow out of his roots.
And the spirit of the Lord shall rest upon him,
   the spirit of wisdom and understanding,
   the spirit of counsel and might,
   the spirit of knowledge and the fear of the Lord,
And his delight shall be in the fear of the Lord. . . .
The wolf shall dwell with the lamb,
   and the leopard shall lie down with the kid,
and the calf and the lion and the fatling together,
   and a little child shall led them.
The cow and the bear shall feed;
   their young shall lie down together;
   and the lion shall eat straw like the ox.
The sucking child shall play over the hole of the asp,
   and the weaned child shall put his hand on the
   adder's den.
They shall not hurt or destroy
   in all my holy mountain;
for the earth shall be full of the knowledge of the
   Lord
   as the waters that cover the sea.

Isaiah 11:1-3, 6-9

Still later, when national crisis became national disaster with the Babylonian captivity, the prophet Ezekiel expressed the hope for restoration in most vivid terms with his vision of the resurrection of the valley of dry bones:

The hand of the Lord was upon me, and he brought me out by the Spirit of the Lord, and set me down in the midst of the valley; it was full of bones. . . . And he said to me, "Son of man, can these bones live?" And I answered, "O Lord God, thou knowest." Again he said to me, "Prophesy to these bones, and say to them, O dry bones, hear the word of the Lord. Thus says the Lord God to these bones: Behold, I will cause breath to enter you, and you shall live. And I will lay sinews upon you, and will cause flesh to come upon you, and cover you with skin, and put breath in you, and you shall live; and you shall know that I am the Lord."

Ezekiel 37:1, 3-6

Also important in Ezekiel is his vision of a new Jerusalem, in which the temple will be rebuilt with all the glory it had in the days of Solomon (chs. 42–48).

These visions are a significant affirmation of the corporate consciousness of ancient Israel. Hopes for the future, as well as present realities, are affirmed with this corporate awareness. At the same time, these visions provided a hope that became a stepping stone toward the idea of restoration and resurrection when later thinkers came to express these views, which gave greater emphasis to the significance of the individual.

In summary, the basic view of Old Testament literature is that humankind is the creation of God. During life, rewards or punishments are the consequence of obedience or disobedience to God. At death, individual existence is no more. The dead depart to the shadowy realm of Sheol. The living retain their memories of the dead and honor the deceased as models and as a part of their sustained corporate identity. In the development of this tradition, there is a shift in emphasis from the family as the focal point of this corporate identity to a focus on the national corporate identity. The visions of renewal, expressed by the prophets, are communications of hope that the power of God will be manifested through the people of God in the restoration of the nation of Israel.

CHAPTER II

Transition to Life
After Death

The Question of the Justice of God

*T*hroughout the Old Testament, the most pervasive
idea is that there is a direct cause and effect between
what one does and one's fate in life. As we have
mentioned, this perspective is often called the
deuteronomic view of history. Briefly stated, it is:
Obey God and prosper; disobey and be judged.
Prosperity or punishment will be experienced in this
life in accordance with the way one has lived. The
best illustration of this idea can be found in the book
of Judges. The success and failure of Israel in her
efforts to conquer the land of Canaan were directly
related to obedience or disobedience to God. When
Israel was faithful to God, she was able to overcome
her enemies. When she went "whoring after other
gods" (Judg. 2:17 KJV), Israel was the victim of op-

pression at the hands of her enemies. This oppression continued until Israel repented. At that point, God would appoint a judge to lead the Israelites from their oppression into a prosperity that would last as long as Israel remained faithful to God. Reward was the direct result of obedience to God; punishment was the result of disobedience. For example, Solomon was rewarded by God for his unselfish obedience. When Solomon became king, God told him in a dream, "Ask what I shall give you" (I Kings 3:5). God was pleased that Solomon asked for "an understanding mind to govern thy people, that I may discern between good and evil" (I Kings 3:9). In response God said to Solomon:

> Because you have asked this, and have not asked for yourself long life or riches or the life of your enemies, but have asked for yourself understanding to discern what is right, behold, I now do according to your word. . . . I give you also what you have not asked, both riches and honor, so that no other king shall compare with you, all your days.
>
> I Kings 3:11-12*a*, 13

An example of punishment for disobedience is seen in the story of Achan. Following the battle of Jericho, the people of Israel were commanded to take "the silver and gold, and the vessels of bronze and of iron" that were captured and put them "into the treasury of the house of the Lord" (Josh. 6:24). However, Achan took some of the "devoted things" for himself. The subsequent defeat at the hands of

the men of Ai is described as the direct punishment
for this misdeed. Achan was then punished according to the demands of God.

> And he who is taken with the devoted things shall be
> burned with fire, he and all that he has, because he
> has transgressed the covenant of the Lord, and
> because he has done a shameful thing in Israel. . . .
> And all Israel stoned him with stones; they burned
> them with fire, and stoned them with stones.
>
> Joshua 7:15, 25

Even though the deuteronomic theology remained
the dominant view, in time there were important
figures in the biblical narrative who began to question
this perspective. Jeremiah, a prophet of the late
seventh and early sixth centuries B.C., is one. Through
his many struggles to proclaim the message of God to
a troubled people in a difficult age, he mused, "Why
does the way of the wicked prosper?" while the
righteous suffer (Jer. 12:1). Note that he did not ask,
"Could it be that the wicked prosper while the
righteous suffer?" His observation is basically that of
many in the twentieth century as well: Why do bad
things happen to good people?

Further reflection on this question is seen in the
writing of Isaiah, the great prophet of the exile (see
Isa. 40–55). Anticipating the liberation of the Jews,
who were in Babylonian captivity, he observes that
Israel has suffered double for all her sins. While his
overall tone is one of hope, his observation seems to

reflect his expectation that there was a deuteronomic balancing of sin and suffering.

The most intense questioning of the deuteronomic view of history in the Old Testament, however, is found in the book of Job. The ancient story of Job was composed in the post-exilic period. The prosperous Job is the topic of a discussion between God and Satan. (The reader should observe that God and Satan are on friendly terms.) Satan, an agent in the heavenly court, does not appear as an adversary of God, a role he takes in later biblical literature. When adversity replaces prosperity for Job, his friends approach, asking what he has done to warrant God's punishing him. He insists that in terms of the law he is a morally upright person. His friends insist that he has shortcomings that he will not admit even to himself. Still, Job declares that he has done nothing to deserve his fate. He suggests:

> My foot has held fast to his steps;
>   I have kept his way and have not turned aside.
> I have not departed from the commandment of his
>   lips;
>   I have treasured in my bosom the words of his
>   mouth.
>
> Job 23:11-12

In the end, Job is forced to acknowledge that God's infinite wisdom is superior to human understanding. The wisdom of God is reflected in the finely tuned realm of nature, in which there seems to be a purpose for everything—the seasons change with rhythm and precision; the mating season of the deer reflects a purposeful order. It just may be that the God who has so carefully designed the universe has an explanation and a purpose for what has happened to Job. One thing is certain, however: The explanation is not the deuteronomic view of history. Life is not so simple! Nevertheless, Job affirms that God is omnipotent and that the divine purpose will prevail.

> I know that thou canst do all things,
> and that no purpose of thine can be thwarted.
> Job 42:2

Whereas Job questions the deuteronomic view of history, the book of Ecclesiastes offers an even more skeptical opinion of the traditional interpretation of rewards and punishments. The author asserts that not only do the righteous and the wicked die, but also the beasts suffer the same fate:

> Moreover I saw under the sun that in the place of justice, even there was wickedness, and in the place of righteousness, even there was wickedness. I said in my heart, God will judge the righteous and the wicked, for he has appointed a time for every matter, and for every work. I said in my heart with regard to the sons of men that God is testing them to show them that they are but beasts. For the fate of the sons of men and the fate of beasts is the same; as one dies, so dies the other. They all have the same breath, and man has no advantage over the beasts; for all is vanity. All go to one place; all are from the dust, and all turn to dust again. Who knows whether the spirit

of man goes upward and the spirit of the beast goes
down to the earth?

Ecclesiastes 3:16-21

In Ecclesiastes 9:1-3, the author affirms more force-
fully that one fate comes to all:

> But all this I laid to heart, examining it all, how the
> righteous and the wise and their deeds are in the
> hand of God; whether it is love or hate man does not
> know. Everything before them is vanity, since one
> fate comes to all, to the righteous and the wicked, to
> the good and the evil, to the clean and the unclean, to
> him who sacrifices and him who does not sacrifice. As
> is the good man, so is the sinner; and he who swears is
> as he who shuns an oath. This is as evil in all that is
> done under the sun, that one fate comes to all; also
> the hearts of men are full of evil, and madness is in
> their hearts while they live, and after that they go to
> the dead.

The question of the justice of God points to an even
more basic concern that seems to trouble the Jews of
the post-exilic period. If the deuteronomic view of
history does not work, then where is the justice of
God? From a logical point of view, there seem to have
been two possibilities. First, God is not just. (The basic
affirmations concerning the character of God were so
deep-rooted that the people simply were not able to
entertain this possibility.) Second, God's justice is
reflected in a manner other than rewards and
punishments in this life. It is as if some were
suggesting that they had been looking in the wrong
direction for an explanation of God's justice. Rather

than look at this life as the realm in which the justice of God is meted out, they began to consider the possibility of life after death as the realm in which this justice would be experienced. (See Job 14:7-14; also Eccles. 9:1-3.)

In this important evolution of thought, the intellectual concepts of cosmic dualism were both influential and helpful. It is on this view of reality that we now focus our attention.

Cosmic Dualism

One is not able to say specifically when cosmic dualism first came to influence the Jews in their thinking. Certainly its influence came to be present during the period of Persian control, around 538–331 B.C. That period is less well known than most in biblical history, in terms of the internal life of the Jews. It is possible to say that we see little evidence of cosmic dualism in 400 B.C., but by 165 B.C. cosmic dualism dominates the book of Daniel and much of Jewish literature beyond that epoch.

Cosmic dualism first appears in the biblical era as a Persian phenomenon, reflecting that religious tradition. It is appropriate to observe, however, that by the time the perspective of cosmic dualism became full-blown in the biblical tradition, the Jews were already under Greek control, Greek thought, and Greek culture, all of which manifested some aspect of cosmic dualism. Greek thinking, therefore, also became a source of dualistic thought among the Jewish people.

What is cosmic dualism? It is the view that the world, or *cosmos,* is characterized by competing and opposite forces, a force for good and a force for evil. These forces are locked in a struggle for control of the cosmos that extends throughout history. Each force has a realm from which it attempts to influence the people of the world, and each has messengers who flit from these respective realms to earth. The struggle is an intense, open-ended one. Evil is as likely to win as is good. In the end, the victorious power will be rewarded with a kingdom, and all who have identified with that power throughout history will share in the reward of that kingdom.

The literature of Judaism in which this dualistic way of thinking is expressed is called *apocalyptic literature.* The book of Daniel (see ch. 7–12) is the best example of apocalyptic literature in the Old Testament; however, it is only one of many examples of this type of literature from this period. Through an intricate system of symbols, numbers, and visions (the Greek word *apocalypsis* means "vision" or "revelation"), apocalyptic literature expresses hope for the people of God, who, though they are oppressed, will nevertheless share in the reward of the kingdom.

This way of thinking was helpful to the Jews because it provided a way of conceptualizing how the justice of God could be manifest at the end of history. This idea also explained their problem of intense suffering in the post-exilic period. Suffering could now be understood as occurring not only because people had done evil, but also because they were on the side of God. However, cosmic dualism also created problems for the Jews because the basic affirmation of Judaism is that "the Lord our God is one" (Deut. 6:4). How were the monotheistic Jews to deal with a view that is in principle dualistic? They did so by adhering to the basic affirmation, "In the beginning God . . . " (Gen. 1:1). God is the first cause, the prime mover, that which is before all others. The traditional view of God in a royal court surrounded by angels was also preserved. According to a later popular tradition, one of the angels rebelled against God and was cast from the heights of heaven. In the book of Isaiah, the Babylonian ruler is the victim of a taunt, which reveals language similar to that used in Canaanite and Babylonian mythology to describe the fall of rebellious creatures in a cosmic struggle:

How you are fallen from heaven,
  O Day Star, son of Dawn!
How you are cut down to the ground,
  you who laid the nations low!
You said in your heart,
  "I will ascend to heaven;
above the stars of God
  I will set my throne on high;
I will sit on the mount of assembly
  in the far north;
I will ascend above the heights of the clouds,
  I will make myself like the Most High."

But you are brought down to Sheol,
to the depths of the Pit.

Isaiah 14:12-15

This fallen king later came to be associated with Satan, whom we have already seen as present with God on a friendly basis, and who came to be regarded as the instigator of sin, having incited David to an act that was displeasing to God (see I Chron. 21:1, 7). To make these two aspects of Satan consistent, "It was necessary to envision a rebellion prior to creation which had resulted in his expulsion" from the heavenly council (Bailey, *Biblical Perspectives on Death*, p. 82). Once this "backward projection" (Bailey, p. 82, note 18) took place, Satan was linked to other references of conflict to which there are only fragmentary references in biblical literature (see Job 7:12; 26:12-13; Ps. 74:13-14; Isa. 27:1). It is this rebellious Satan who becomes the personification of evil and, as such, is identified as the force of evil. Thus God has been reaffirmed in monotheistic terms, and on a secondary, day-to-day level there is also the ongoing intense struggle between the force of good (God) and the force of evil (Satan). The closer history moves toward its end, the more bitter the struggle becomes. Each force has its messengers to act as intermediaries with the inhabitants of the world. Increasingly, however, the neutral or positive word for messenger was used in relation to the messengers of God—*angels*. The messengers of Satan came to be called demons. As the end of history approached, there was still the idea that there would be a reward for the victorious power and for all who have identified with that victorious power. The reward was called the kingdom of God. Suddenly, this struggle was no longer an open-ended one! In the beginning is God and in the end is the kingdom of God. The open-endedness of earlier dualism had been replaced with a confidence that in the end God would be in control.

How shall we know when this victorious end is approaching? One of the signs of the end is that the conflicts of the present age will intensify. When the circumstances of life become so unbearable that even God's faithful cannot endure, then God will intervene, bringing an end to history.

By adopting a modified cosmic dualism, the Jews were able to affirm their monotheistic belief in God and at the same time to find a mental construct that helped to contend with the question of the justice of God. It is this latter question that seems to be the primary focus of the first full-blown expression of this modified cosmic dualism in Daniel. The book of Daniel was written in the Maccabean period (around 167–164 B.C.), during the struggle of the Jews against Antiochus IV Epiphanes. Faithful Jews had been persecuted for their loyalty to the Torah, the law of their ancestors. Daniel and his friends are models of encouragement to the Jews in this stressful situation. His dreams attest to the fact that the power of God will prevail. In the end, the justice of God will be established by God's might and those who have been faithful will be rewarded. Those who have persecuted the faithful will, likewise, receive their reward. In Daniel 12 there is a pointed focus on those who await their fate:

> At that time shall arise Michael, the great prince who has charge of your people. And there shall be a time of trouble, such as never has been since there was a nation till that time; but at that time your people shall be delivered, every one whose name shall be found written in the book. And many of those who sleep in the dust of the earth shall awake, some to everlasting life, and some to shame and everlasting contempt. And those who are wise shall shine like the brightness of the firmament; and those who turn many to righteousness, like the stars for ever and ever.
>
> Daniel 12:1-3

This passage in Daniel is the earliest affirmation in the biblical tradition of a clear assertion of belief in some type of life after death, with rewards and punishments. It is noteworthy that the deuteronomic view is still operative. In Daniel, however, rewards and punishments are manifested beyond death, rather than being revealed immediately in this life.

The Furniture of Heaven and Hell

Once the Jewish community of faith had accepted the idea of life after death with rewards and punishments, a natural question was: What is it like? It is as though the people said, "What is the very best that we can imagine? What is the very worst we can imagine?" What was the very best they could imagine? In the post-exilic context in which the Jewish community of faith was struggling for survival, Jerusalem had been restored, but without the grandeur of the royal city of David and Solomon or the glory envisioned by Ezekiel. The most splendid vision imaginable for the afterlife was to have a new Jerusalem, adorned by the presence of God and precious stones.

The book of Ezekiel contains the recollection of an early tradition in which humankind was present with God on "the holy mountain of God" (Ezek. 28:14):

> You were the signet of perfection,
>   full of wisdom
>   and perfect in beauty.
> You were in Eden, the garden of God;
>   every precious stone was your covering,
> carnelian, topaz, and jasper,
>   chrysolite, beryl, and onyx,
> sapphire, carbuncle, and emerald;
>   and wrought in gold were your settings
>   and your engravings.
> On the day that you were created
>   they were prepared.
> With an anointed guardian cherub I placed you;
>   you were on the holy mountain of God.
>   Ezekiel 28:11-14

The book of Isaiah, in anticipating the restoration of Jerusalem, uses a description of precious stones that has similarities to that earlier tradition.

> O afflicted one, storm-tossed, and not comforted,
> behold, I will set your stones in antimony,
> and lay your foundations with sapphires.

— 5 3 —

I will make your pinnacles of agate,
    your gates of carbuncles,
    and all your wall of precious stones.

Isaiah 54:11-12

It was in this luxurious setting that the Jews placed their long-held view of God's being in a royal court flanked by cherubim and seated on a throne. It was this image that had been expressed in the Holy of Holies in the Temple of Solomon. This long-held image also provided the background for the accounts of creation, in which the writers seem to presuppose God in a royal court addressing the celestial attendants (see Gen. 1:1–3:24).

This composite vision of the heavenly realm seems to draw together the view of God as king and ruler, along with the idea of an ideal Jerusalem. The lack of a Davidic leader in the exilic and post-exilic periods of history heightened the need to express the idea of an ideal Jerusalem. Ezekiel expressed the view of a restored Jerusalem, of which he is given a preview from a mountaintop in a vision (Ezek. 40:2). A vision of the restored Jerusalem is further expressed in Isaiah 65:17-18:

For behold, I create new heavens
    and a new earth;
and the former things shall not be remembered
    or come into mind.
But be glad and rejoice for ever
    in that which I create;
for behold, I create Jerusalem a rejoicing,
    and her people a joy.

In numerous passages the holy mountain of God (that is, Jerusalem) will be established in a lasting manner (compare Isa. 11:9; 27:13; 56:7; 65:25; Joel 3:17). Though these passages focus primarily on the restoration of Jerusalem in the post-exilic period, the connection of the new Jerusalem with the creation of a new heaven (see Isa. 65:17-18, above) provided imagery that in later periods was transformed into a concept of heaven, shaped almost totally from and by the cultural and historical context of this era (see Gal. 4:26).

What is the worst that they could imagine? On the edge of Jerusalem was a valley that was used as the town garbage heap. From the precipice above, debris could be dumped into the ravine, where it smoldered incessantly. The worst that could be imagined was to be cast into this Valley of Hinnom and to burn forever, no longer only smoldering but consumed by the raging flames of fire and brimstone. It is no accident that the Greek word for this fiery location, or hell, is *Gehenna,* a transliteration of the Hebrew word for the Valley of Hinnom. At some point along the way, the image of the valley of fire was combined with the concept of the pit of Sheol. This visual combination provided the even more devastating image of a pit of fire from which there was no escape—ever. This concept served as the basis for what we now call *hell.*

Intertestamental Period

Following the affirmation of Daniel 12 that there will be a resurrection of many, some to be rewarded and some to be punished, there is a rapid development of ideas about life after death. Both the historical events with which the Jews had to deal—persecution and martyrdom—and the impact of certain Greek ways of thinking about the soul helped to shape the ideas of this period.

The conceptual developments of the intertestamental period are documented in the literature of the Apocrypha and the Pseudepigrapha, Jewish writings of this period which were not included in the Bible. The historical reality that many Christians, especially in the Protestant traditions, have abandoned use of this literature has made it difficult for many to trace the evolution of various religious ideas during this era. Fortunately, increasing awareness of the Apocrypha and Pseudepigrapha is a move toward a more complete understanding of the intertestamental period, and thus provides a link between Old Testament ideas on various topics and what is found in the New Testament.

The persecution of the Jews in the Maccabean period (167–164 B.C.) gave rise and emphasis to the feeling that the faithful were living in the last days, when the victory would belong to God and God's faithful people. At the same time that there was confidence in final victory with God in the ultimate struggle of history, it became necessary to deal with the question of what happens to those who do not live until the end, those who had died for the cause. The preoccupation with this question suggests that the affirmation of death as the final end for human beings had become a theological problem needing to be resolved (see Bailey, p. 77). There was no longer the contentment to say with the people of old, "And he died and was gathered to his fathers."

The problem of affirming God's justice in this world, an issue with which the community of faith had wrestled since the exile, became a central issue for reflection. The resulting focus on life after death led to the development of numerous ideas in the intertestamental period. As in Daniel, the most immediate concern of this period was with the fate of those who had suffered despite their faithfulness to the Torah. In the Wisdom of Solomon, the righteous man is exalted in a heavenly courtroom, while his former persecutor is condemned (see Wisd. of Sol. 2–5). "Then the righteous man will stand with great confidence in the presence of those who have afflicted him, and those who make light of his labors" (Wisd. of Sol. 5:1); "They [the unrighteous] will be left utterly dry and barren, and they will suffer anguish, and the memory of them shall perish" (Wisd. of Sol. 4:19).

In contrast to the unrighteous who experience death because they belong to the realm of the devil (Wisd. of Sol. 2:24), "The souls of the righteous are in the hand of God, and no torment will ever touch them" (Wisd. of Sol. 3:1). "But the righteous man, though he die early, will be at rest" (Wisd. of Sol. 4:7). Further, it is stated,

But the righteous live forever,
　and their reward is with the Lord;
　the Most High takes care of them.
Therefore they will receive a glorious crown.
Wisdom of Solomon 5:15-16

In II Maccabees 7, seven brothers were condemned to death because of their faithfulness to the Torah. Their mother, forced to watch the torture of her sons, and before she likewise perished, affirmed her belief in their restoration in the resurrection. The hope of this era is reflected in the words uttered to the persecutors by two of the sons prior to their death: "You dismiss us from this present life, but the King of the universe will raise us up to an everlasting renewal of life, because we have died for his laws" (II Macc. 7:9). The clearest affirmation is that those who have died in faithfulness to God shall not have died in vain. Their faithfulness to God will be rewarded. This hope is not only true for the martyr, but also for others who have endured this life without reward. In response to the oppression of the poor, Enoch 92–105 depicts the reversal of roles that will occur in the afterlife. Having affirmed that one's lot in this life is not a sign of one's eternal plight, the writer affirms reward for the righteous and punishment for the sinner in the hereafter. Divine justice is a function of the future life, rather than the present life. Having warned the unrighteous of his fate, Enoch says,

Fear ye not, ye souls of righteousness,
And be hopeful ye that have died in righteousness.

And grieve not if your soul into Sheol has descended
  in grief,
And that in your life your body fared not according
  to your goodness,
But wait for the day of the judgement of sinners
And for the day of cursing and chastisement.

Enoch 102:4-5

Of the evil person the author of Enoch says,
"Nevertheless they perished and became as though
they had not been, and their spirits descended into
Sheol in tribulation" (Enoch 102:11).

In great contrast to the fate of the wicked is the role
of the righteous, as described by Enoch:

Now, therefore, I swear to you, the righteous, by the
  glory of the Great and Honoured and Mighty One
  in dominion, and by His greatness I swear to you.
I know a mystery
And have read the heavenly tablets,
And have seen the holy books,
And have found written therein and inscribed
  regarding them:
That all goodness and joy and glory
  are prepared for them,
And written down for the spirits of those who have
  died in righteousness,
And that manifold good shall be given to you in
  recompense for your labours,
And that your lot is abundantly beyond the lot of the
  living.

Enoch 103:1-3

In Daniel, the resurrection of many to reward and
punishment represented an effort to deal with the

oppressed and the oppressors. As reflection on life after death became less directly an expression of concern for the fate of the martyred and oppressed, there was a tendency to focus more broadly on the idea of a universal resurrection. Increasingly in his period, there was the question later asked of Paul by those in the church at Corinth: "With what kind of body do they come?" (I Cor. 15:35).

On this question, the intertestamental literature expresses a diversity of ideas reflecting a growing influence of dualistic ways of thinking about what it means to be a person. The Greek way of thinking, whose influence can be seen in this period, views human existence in terms of anthropological dualism. In this pattern of thinking, the essence of a person is the "soul," which may have an existence separate from the body. Note that this concept is in stark contrast to the basic Old Testament view already observed. In that early view, a person is a "living being" for whom body and *nephesh* are inseparable aspects. One cannot be a person without both body and nephesh. With the development of this dualistic pattern of thought, it became possible to reflect on a separate fate beyond death for the body and for the soul, or spirit, as this dimension of the person is sometimes called. In Jubilees 23:31 the "spirits" of the righteous will experience much joy while the bodies are relegated to the earth.

> And their bones shall rest in the earth,
> And their spirits shall have much joy.
> Jubilees 23:31

In Enoch 102:4–103:8 there is an extreme dualism, in which the spirits of the righteous (some texts say "souls") "come to life" while those of sinners burn in Sheol.

> Know ye, that their souls will be made to descend into Sheol
> And they shall be wretched in their great tribulation.
> And into darkness and chains and a burning flame where there is grievous judgement shall your spirits enter.
>
> Enoch 103:7-8

Note that in this pasage Sheol seems to be the final place of judgment, whereas in Enoch 102:5 (quoted above) it is the place of waiting until the day of judgment. It is also noteworthy that while the text speaks of souls (or spirits) going to Sheol, there seems to be the assumption of sufficient corporeal substance to experience the impact of darkness, chains, and burning flame. Other passages speak more directly of the resurrection of the body. In the passages referred to above in II Maccabees 7, there is the repeated comment on being "revived" (v. 9); on the restoration of hands and tongue marred by persecution (v. 11); on being "raised up" (v. 4); and even on restoring the breath of life (v. 23). The emphasis of this passage, which is typically Hebraic, is an obvious effort to affirm the faithfulness of God to those whose bodies have experienced martyrdom. Fourth Maccabees 9–18 reworks the tradition of II Maccabees 7, replacing the emphasis of the resurrection of the body with a focus on the immortality of an incorruptible soul that is guided by reason. Fourth Maccabees concludes with the affirmation: "But the sons of Abraham, with their victorious mother, are gathered together unto the place of their ancestors, having received pure and immortal souls from God, to whom be glory for ever and ever. Amen" (IV Macc. 18:23-24).

Second Esdras 7 views the soul as participating in a resurrection at the end of time. This resurrection will be followed by a universal judgment in which some are invited to delight and rest and some to fire and torment (II Esd. 7:31-44).

The references in Daniel 12:2 to the resurrection of "those who sleep" and to the righteous who grieve in Sheol in Enoch 102–103 may suggest an intermediate state between death and the final resurrection and judgment, whatever its form may be.

The prevalence of ideas on life after death that developed during the late post-exilic period reflects the growing concern with the topic in the intertestamental period. From the evidence cited, one could conclude that belief in life after death with rewards and punishments had become an accepted fact in the Judaism of this period. However, this conclusion is not altogether accurate. There were strong differences of opinion and lively debate on the issue between two of the most influential groups within Judaism, the Sadducees and the Pharisees. The Sadducees saw the Torah (i.e., Genesis through Deuteronomy) as God's primary revelation. If a theological truth were not at least implied in the Torah, it held no sway with the Sadducees. Thus they are described in Mark 12:18 as believing that there is no resurrection. The Pharisees were a group that emerged primarily in the aftermath of the Maccabean struggle. For them, new theological truths were continually being revealed. Among these new truths was the affirmation of the resurrection of the dead with rewards and punishments. As Pharisaic Judaism strengthened in the intertestamental and New Testament eras, so did acceptance of their ideas concerning life after death. The ideas about life after death which developed in the late Old Testament and intertestamental period are in marked contrast to the views of the earlier Old Testament period. They both provide the setting for and have more in common with the teachings of the New Testament, on which we now focus our attention.

CHAPTER III

New Testament Views of Life After Death

*I*n examining the New Testament writings, it appears that the belief in life after death with rewards and punishments was a presupposition of the early Christian community. The affirmation of the resurrection of Jesus, as well as the assertion of the theme of renewal in contemporary Judaism, was the basis of the hope for resurrection. The belief in the early *parousia* (i.e., the idea that Jesus would return soon to consummate the kingdom) is reflected in several different strands of the New Testament writings. New Testament writers focus on the parousia with confidence that the end will bring with it rewards for God's people and punishments for God's enemies.

It is interesting and valuable to compare various New Testament writings on this topic. It is also important to concentrate as clearly as possible on ideas about life after death, separating them as much as possible from related ideas of the parousia, the early consummation of the kingdom of God, and the end of the present age.

The Gospels

The most obvious technical problem in looking at the Gospels is to separate the views and attitudes of Jesus from those of the Gospel writers and of the early church. It is, however, important to affirm that both the attitudes of Jesus and those of the early church are a part of the Gospels as they reflect the life of the early Christian communities; therefore, an effort will be made to look at clues for a view of life after death that are reflected in the Gospels as they stand.

Especially in examining the Gospels, it is not an easy task to separate the strong emphasis on the coming of the kingdom from affirmations of life after death. In attempting to understand the advent of the kingdom, there are several aspects of the problem one must comprehend. First, there is the affirmation that the kingdom is an immediate reality as well as a future possibility. Second, the kingdom manifests itself in both communal and individual expressions. It will be helpful, however, to comment on the coming of the kingdom so as to demonstrate the difference between the two. Futhermore, it will be helpful to separate our discussion of the Synoptic Gospels (Matthew, Mark, and Luke) from the discussion of the Gospel of John, so that the differences between them will become more obvious.

The Synoptic Gospels

In the Synoptic Gospels, Jesus is portrayed as expressing the expectation of the early end of history and the unprecedented manifestation of the reign of God, including rewards for God's people and punishments for God's enemies. In this affirmation Jesus shared the primary eschatological view (understanding of the end or goal of history) that was characteristic of Judaism in his day. The primary difference in the view expressed in the Synoptic Gospels from that characteristic of Judaism in the New Testament era is the emphasis on Jesus, himself, as the one who would usher in the kingdom of God and the inclusion of non-Jews in this kingdom. The coming of the kingdom is expressed primarily in apocalyptic language that had come to be characteristic of intertestamental expressions of the end of time. Mark and Luke usually refer to the coming of "the kingdom of God" (e.g., Mark 1:14; Luke 7:28). Matthew, on the other hand, is more likely to speak of "the kingdom of heaven" (e.g., Matt. 4:7; 5:20). This use of "heaven" by Matthew is in all probability grounded in the Jewish tradition of reticence to pronounce the name of God, and Matthew was writing for Christians of Jewish background. Therefore, when Matthew, in particular, speaks of heaven, one should not automatically assume that he is speaking of life after death. He is often speaking of the presence of God and the present commitment to God (see Matt. 6:20).

Jesus' expectation of an early advent of the kingdom of God is reflected in his preaching: "The time is fulfilled, and the kingdom of God is at hand; repent, and believe in the gospel" (Mark 1:15). Jesus apparently expected the end of the present age to be very near, and clearly Mark interpreted that end as having an immediate impact on Jesus' work and the work of his followers. "Truly, I say to you, there are some standing here who will not taste death before they see that the kingdom of God has come with power" (Mark 9:1; compare Matt. 11:23). In Luke, the presence of the kingdom is expressed directly: "The kingdom of God is in the midst of you" (Luke 17:21).

While these and other passages in the Synoptic Gospels portray the kingdom of God in present terms, it is not possible to interpret the Synoptic Gospels as a whole without recognizing that there is also a future dimension to what is being proclaimed. These affirmations of the future relate more directly to assumptions and affirmations about life after death. Many of Jesus' sayings about the future kingdom, with its rewards and punishments, are expressed in parable and metaphor.

In Mark 12:18-27 Jesus is confronted by the Sadducees, who are described as saying there is no resurrection. Their question about the biblically sanctioned marriages of a woman who had been the wife of seven brothers in succession (according to the tradition of levirate marriage) seems to be designed to show how ridiculous the whole question of resurrection is. Jesus' response to this "entrapment" question, however, affirms a belief in life after death. He asserts that "when they rise from the dead, they neither marry nor are given in marriage, but are like angels in heaven" (Mark 12:25). His response suggests that resurrection life is not a continuation of the normal physical experience. It is, rather, an affirmation of the continuing power and presence of God, who is "not the God of the dead, but of the living" (Mark 12:27).

When the rich young ruler approaches Jesus (Mark 10:17), his question is, "Good Teacher, what must I do to inherit eternal life?" While the phrase *eternal life* has many possible implications, its use, in conjunction with the idea of the resurrection of the dead, in intertestamental literature suggests that it refers here to life in the age to come. Futhermore, Jesus speaks about the young ruler's "rewards in heaven" if he will go beyond the demands of the law and sell what he has to give to the poor. An extension of this idea is expressed in the following passage, in which Jesus says that those who have sacrificed will receive the reward of eternal life in the age to come:

> Truly, I say to you, there is no one who has left house or brothers or sisters or mother or father or children or lands, for my sake and for the gospel, who will not receive a hundredfold now in this time, houses and brothers and sisters and mothers and children and

lands, with persecutions, and in the age to come eternal life.

Mark 10:29-30

In Luke's parable of the rich man and Lazarus (Luke 16:19-31), the idea and imagery of life after death with rewards and punishments is reinforced. This parable also emphasizes the theme of the reversal of roles after death, which came to be prevalent in intertestamental literature. The fate one had experienced on earth would be reversed, or adjusted, so as to achieve justice. The rich man is told, "Son, remember that you in your lifetime received your good things; but now he [Lazarus] is comforted here, and you are in anguish" (Luke 16:25). The anguish the rich man experienced was "in Hades, being in torment" (Luke 16:23). His situation is further described in verse 24: "For I am in anguish in this flame." His discomfort is compounded by the fact that he "saw Abraham far off and Lazarus in his bosom" (Luke 16:23). Even with the development of apocalyptic imagery present in this parable, the collective image of the comfort of being in the presence of one's forebears in death remains.

The parable of the last judgment in Matthew 25:31-46, while showing that the basis for judgment is what one does on earth, uses apocalyptic imagery to describe a judgment at the end of history, in which there will be everlasting rewards and punishments. The assertion, "Before him will be gathered all the nations" (Matt. 25:32), suggests that this is to be a universal judgment. The images of "the kingdom prepared for you from the foundation of the world" (Matt. 25:34) and "eternal fire prepared for the devil and his angels" (Matt. 25:41) convey divine approval and condemnation.

In Luke 23:43, Jesus proclaims to one of the criminals who was crucified with him, "Today you will be with me in Paradise." This passage is often regarded as a clear statement of Jesus' view of what follows death. Perhaps more important in this context is the affirmation of forgiveness, expressed by Jesus, but the clear implication is a belief in life after death that begins immediately.

In general, the affirmations of the Synoptic Gospels, pointing in the direction of future aspects of the kingdom and life after death, are expressed in highly symbolic apocalyptic language. They are more concerned with proclaiming the power of God and Jesus than they are with making explicit a view of life after death. What is stated about life after death is often based more on assumption and implication than on explicit and direct application. This assumption is clearly that life after death is a reality.

The Gospel of John

In the Gospel of John, there is a shift away from the apocalyptic imagery of resurrection at the end of the age to an emphasis on the gift of eternal life as a present reality. The kingdom is, therefore, not so much an externally demonstrable reality as it is an inward reality, transforming the life of an individual. The repeated promises of life in John have an overtone suggesting the quality of life. Abundance of life (i.e., new life) is affirmed as a promise to those who are living already. In the prologue to the Gospel of John, the author says of Jesus, "In him was life, and the life was the light of men" (John 1:4). Later he affirms, "That whoever believes in him [Jesus] may have eternal life" (John 3:15). The present aspect of this gift is strongly affirmed, "Truly, truly, I say to you, he who hears my word and believes him who sent me, has eternal life" (John 5:24). Likewise, the judgment of God is a present reality:

> He who believes in him is not condemned; he who does not believe is condemned already, because he has not believed in the name of the only Son of God. And this is the judgment, that the light has come into the world, and men loved darkness rather than light, because their deeds were evil.
>
> John 3:18-19
>
> He who believes in the Son has eternal life; he who does not obey the Son shall not see life.
>
> John 3:36

The raising of Lazarus in John 11 prefigures the resurrection of Jesus. More importantly, however, the story of the raising of Lazarus declares the present reality of the power of Jesus to give life *now*. In the context of the narrative, Martha asserts her belief in a resurrection on the last day. She observes, "I know that he will rise again in the resurrection at the last day" (John 11:24). Jesus focuses attention on present and future (ongoing) reality, which is

— 7 1 —

life-giving to both Lazarus and Martha. "I am the resurrection and the life; he who believes in me, though he die, yet shall he live, and whoever believes in me shall never die" (John 11:25-26). The gift of life in the present is further emphasized by John. The beginning of the new life now is, however, a guarantee of a life beyond death.

The present life-giving power of Jesus is also affirmed in John 14:1-7. In this final discourse, Jesus is preparing the apostles for life abundant after his death. The coming of a Counselor is not only a future event, but also a present reality. This present reality, this Counselor, will "be with you forever" (John 14:16). This Counselor, identified as the "Spirit of truth" (John 14:17) and "the Holy Spirit" (John 14:26), "dwells with you, and will be in you" (John 4:17). It is not necessary to wait for the parousia, that is, the return of Jesus. John shifted the emphasis to stress present reality as the starting point of a life that is true, abundant, and eternal. In making this strong emphasis on the present, John has not denied the elements of a future life; he has simply not stressed them. However, a dimension of futurity remains:

> Let not your heart be troubled; believe in God, believe also in me. In my Father's house are many rooms; if it were not so, would I have told you that I go to prepare a place for you? And when I go and prepare a place for you, I will come again and will take you to myself, that where I am you may be also.
> John 14:1-3

Despite the persistence of passages like this one, John chooses to focus on life here and now. His emphasis is on the indwelling presence of God. "If a man loves me, he will keep my word, and my Father will love him, and we will come to him and make our home with him," (John 14:23). The eternal is in the present, a present that extends into the future for those who have been united with God, as Jesus and God are united. John does not choose to speculate on the mysteries of the future.

Paul

For Paul, the expectation of an early end to the present age was as strong as it was for the earlier church. In his correspondence with the church at Thessalonica, Paul seems to have stressed the imminence of the end with such fervor that Christians there were afraid that those who had already died might have missed out on the glories of the parousia (I Thess. 4:13) A similar emphasis on the urgent expectation of the end is expressed in I Corinthians 15, "We shall not all sleep [die], but we shall all be changed" (I Cor. 15:51). Paul shared the then present Jewish belief that the coming of the Messiah would usher in the age of the kingdom. With others in the early church, Paul wrestled with the question of how Jesus could be proclaimed the Christ while history was still ongoing. His answer was that the end was to occur in two stages. The first entails the gift of the spirit, "He who has prepared us for this very thing is God, who has given us the Spirit as a guarantee" (II Cor. 5:5). The second stage is the fruition of the day of resurrection and judgment, prefigured in the resurrection of Jesus, which is the model of that glory to be experienced by all on that last day (I Cor. 15).

In I Corinthians 15, Paul has the most thorough statement of his view of life after death. When Paul first proclaimed the gospel to those in the synagogue in Corinth, he had expressed himself in the resurrection tradition he had inherited from others in the church. He asserted, "I delivered to you as of first importance what I also received" (I Cor. 15:3). This is a formula for describing that which was fixed in the proclamation of the church. The focus of this proclamation is the resurrection of Jesus Christ. To the list of earlier witnesses of the resurrected Lord, Paul added his experience: "Last of all, as to one untimely born, he appeared also to me" (I Cor. 15:8). This proclamation was formulated and passed on in a Jewish conceptual context, which presupposed a person as a living being, animated by the Spirit of God. The only way to comprehend and to speak of the continuation of one's personal existence was to speak of the continuation of the bodily presence of that person—a bodily presence still animated. The Jews simply had never known any person who did not have a body! Therefore, if one were to talk of the resurrection of Jesus or of the believer, it had to be in terms of the resurrection of the body.

As people of Greek culture and Greek thinking became a part of the Christian community, they brought with them their own conceptual orientation. When they heard the proclamation, "We shall all be raised," they were troubled. For the Greeks, the essence of the person was the soul. The body dies, disintegrates, and is no longer in a recognizable form. The soul, which is immortal, has an existence independent of the body. Any continued personal existence is expressed in terms of the immortality of the soul.

When Paul proclaimed his faith in the resurrection of Jesus and his hope that Jesus would be the first fruit of the resurrection of the dead (I Cor. 15:20), he was misunderstood because of the differences between Hebrew and Greek concepts of the essence of personal existence. It is in the context of this misunderstanding that Paul addresses the questions of I Corinthians 15. He did not abandon his affirmation of the centrality of the resurrection. Rather, he continued to affirm that, just as surely as Jesus was raised from the dead, so we all shall be raised. His answer turned to a consideration of the form of the resurrection. In I Corinthians 15:35 Paul asked the rhetorical questions, "How are the dead raised? With what kind of body do they come?"

In his answer Paul begins with the analogy of a grain of wheat that is planted in the ground (I Cor. 15:35). The planted seed will emerge with a new form, a new body. Without using the analogy of a grain of wheat, he expresses a similar idea of resurrection in I Thessalonians 4:16-18 when he asserts that on the day of resurrection "the dead in Christ shall rise first."

Some scholars have interpreted Paul as meaning that the dead will lie dormant until the day of resurrection, when they will be raised. Support for this interpretation can be gleaned from some passages in intertestamental literature. Some people understand Paul as accepting the view that there will be a period of dormancy between death and resurrection on the last day. A more helpful understanding of Paul is to see him as answering his own questions: "How are the dead raised? With what sort of body do they come?" Paul does not appear to be attempting to establish a timetable for events at the end of history. Rather, his emphasis is on the transformation that he asserts will occur after death. This view is supported by his affirmation in Philippians 1:19-26. In this passage, his concern is with the advantages of life over death:

> For to me to live is Christ, and to die is gain. If it is to be life in the flesh, that means fruitful labor for me. Yet which I shall choose I cannot tell. I am hard pressed between the two. My desire is to depart and be with Christ, for that is far better.
>
> Philippians 1:21-22

This passage suggests the immediacy of being with Christ. How, then, does Paul answer his question? His emphasis is on transformation, for that which is planted in death emerges with a new form, a new body, but it retains the same essence. In Paul's analogy of the grain of wheat, that form transcending death will be as different as a stalk of wheat is from a grain of wheat. Even though Paul continues to use the word *body* to describe the entity that emerges from this transformation, it appears that he is talking about the essence of the person (a usage of *body* common to Paul). That essence of the person is still present and is manifest in a new form. What remains, Paul believes, is not flesh (the words for "body" and "flesh" are different in Greek).

Perhaps there is a clue for what he intends in another passage, in which he uses *bodies*. In Romans 12:1, he admonishes his hearers to "present your bodies as a living sacrifice." The plea is for them to present themselves—their essential beings—as living sacrifices. If we understand Paul in I Corinthians 15 to be saying that the same essential being, or self, is retained, then we can more easily grasp his meaning. That "self" that was once manifest in physical form shall now have a spiritual form. There is a continuity; yet "we shall be changed" (I Cor. 15:54). That which will be raised will be a "spiritual body," or a "spiritual self."

Paul also addresses this transformation in II Corinthians 4:16–5:5. Here he uses language that is different, because he speaks of "our outer nature" and "our inner nature" (II Cor. 4:16); the "transient" and the "eternal" (II Cor. 4:18); and "the earthly tent" and a building from God, "a house not made with hands, eternal in the heavens" (II Cor. 5:1). Despite the differences in language, the emphasis is the same as in I Corinthians 15. The essential being will be continued, and the new "spiritual self" will be eternal.

We need to be careful that we do not modernize Paul. While for most the phrase "spiritual body" may suggest a contradiction in terms or a mixing of incompatible words or concepts, that is not the case with Paul. Even though it appears that for Paul the transformed self is no longer flesh, his reference to the "spiritual body" leaves the impression that, after the transformation, the remaining being has some degree of "corporeality," or bodily form, that we may not traditionally associate with a "spiritual self." It is difficult to grasp his main affirmation of the body as self and not lose what is an undeniable Jewish grasping after the concrete, which Paul retains. For Paul, that continuing essence will have a form suitable to spiritual existence: "This perishable nature must put on the imperishable, and this mortal nature must put on immortality" (I Cor. 15:53). For Paul, death is not the end:

> "Death is swallowed up in victory,
> O death, where is thy victory?
> O death, where is thy sting? . . ."
> Thanks be to God, who gives us victory through our Lord Jesus Christ.
>
> I Corinthians 15:54-55, 57

When Paul says in I Corinthians 15, "We shall be raised" and "We shall be changed," he is speaking completely within the context of the Christian community, and what he says is, therefore, to be taken as only an affirmation for the Christian community. Similarly, in I Thessalonians 4, Paul addresses only those who are in the context of the Christian community. There he asserts that "the dead in Christ will [be raised!] rise first," and then those who remain alive shall be joined with them in the air. The resurrection that Paul speaks of so confidently is a resurrection for Christians. Paul does not address the question of a general resurrection. His concern is with the hope that is an outgrowth of life in Christ Jesus. This hope is grounded in the experience of the union of the Christian with God through Christ. Thus for Paul the ultimate affirmation of life after death is this union with God or Christ. This belief is similar to his affirmation of the relationship of the Christian with God through Christ in the present life. A phrase frequently used by Paul to describe that relationship is "in Christ." The culmination of his hope for the Christian after death, in I Thessalonians 4, is the hope to be eternally with the Lord: "We shall always be with the Lord" (I Thess. 4:17).

The ultimate affirmation of Pauline theology is the doxology of Romans 8, which proclaims that nothing—not even death—can separate us from the love of God.

Who shall separate us from the love of Christ? Shall tribulation, or distress, or persecution, or famine, or nakedness, or peril, or sword?

No, in all these things we are more than conquerors through him who loved us. For I am sure that neither death, nor life, nor angels, nor principalities, nor things present, nor things to come, nor powers, nor height, nor depth, nor anything else in all creation, will be able to separate us from the love of God in Christ Jesus our Lord.

Romans 8:35, 37-39

Paul's ultimate hope for life after death is to be united with God. Though his affirmations are couched in apocalyptic language, he is unwavering in his assertion of a continuing spiritual existence with God.

Revelation

The book of Revelation is commonly regarded as focusing primarily on when the world will end. The main thrust of the book of Revelation is, however, on the struggles of Christians experiencing persecution. Like all apocalyptic literature, its primary concern is to offer a word of encouragement to those who are involved in the persecution and to assure them that their faithfulness will be rewarded, for in the end God and God's purpose will be victorious.

Most of the elaborate system of images and symbols in Revelation has at least partial parallelism in the vast array of apocalyptic literature of the intertestamental and New Testament era. The center of focus is on the cosmic struggle between the forces of good and evil. In Revelation, this struggle is expressed totally in terms of Christian theology and testimony. Jesus, the Lamb of God, is the agent of victory. As is the case with all apocalyptic literature, the basic question is how it is to be interpreted. Is it as a blueprint of how history will come to an end, or is it a highly symbolic affirmation that whenever and however history ends, God will be in control and those who have been faithful to God will be rewarded, while those who have sided against God will be confronted by divine judgment?

The apocalyptic vision of John is an affirmation that the power and purpose of God cannot be thwarted in history. Even with the apparently meaningless suffering of those who are faithful, God's power will be ultimate. History will move toward its *eschaton*—its goal, its end. As noted in the earlier discussion of the Synoptic Gospels, this end is not merely chronological. That which is God's purpose can be expressed within history as well as at the end of history. The elaborate symbols of Revelation are an effort to express with confidence that the power and purpose of God will prevail. The God "who is and who was and who is to come" is "the ruler of kings on earth" (Rev. 1:4-5). God has power even over "Death and Hades" (Rev. 1:18). Though there may be temporary control by the forces of evil, God's purpose will prevail.

God's victory over evil is expressed in imagery reminiscent of Isaiah and Ezekiel. A new Jerusalem is described in glorious detail (see Rev. 4:1-11; 5:11; 14:2, 3; 21:1-21). God in all divine splendor will reign supreme. It is important, however, to observe that this new Jerusalem is not a place to which one escapes from earth. This new Jerusalem is a reality that descends upon the faithful.

> And he said to me, "It is done! I am the Alpha and the Omega, the beginning and the end. To the thirsty I will give from the fountain of the water of life without payment. He who conquers shall have this heritage, and I will be his God and he shall be my son. . . ."
> And in the spirit he carried me away to a great, high mountain, and showed me the holy city Jerusalem coming down out of heaven from God.
>
> Revelation 21:6-7, 10

When the purpose of God prevails, there will be a renewal of the ideal that has been expressed from much earlier in the biblical tradition. The dwelling place of God will be among humanity, for God "is not God of the dead, but of the living" (Mark 12:27). The final proclamation of the biblical tradition is that the ultimate goal of God for the end of the age is renewal. This is an affirmation of life. Herein lies our hope. God's purpose is greater than any one of us. That purpose shall transcend even death.

When seen in this light, Revelation is more a book about overcoming the powers of evil in this life than about life after death. The imagery of apocalypticism speaks of a victory of God that is so complete as to renew creation. Those people who are faithful to God will share in that victory—even in death—for the forces of evil have no power over the death of the spirit ("the second death"; see Rev. 20:6). Those people who are faithless have by their own deeds separated themselves from God (see Rev. 20:12). They shall not experience the new Jerusalem, which comes down to become the dwelling place of God and those who are faithful.

While the primary thrust of Revelation is not on life after death, there are, nevertheless, affirmations about the fate of martyrs. As the fifth seal is broken in Revelation 6, the author says: "I saw under the altar the souls of those who have been slain for the word of God and for the witness they had borne" (Rev. 6:9). Though this imagery may only suggest that these souls are beneath the altar because they have been sacrificed, the force of this vision suggests that the emphasis is on the martyrs' presence with God. Those who have been faithful even unto death have a special proximity to God after death.

Revelation 20 offers a similar affirmation: "Also I saw the souls of those who had been beheaded for their testimony to Jesus and for the word of God, and who had not worshiped the beast or its image and had not received its mark on their foreheads or their hands" (Rev. 20:4-5). These faithful are already present with God and Christ and already share in the victory and judgment with them (Rev. 20:1-6). The hope of this same presence with God and Christ awaits all who remain faithful. They shall reign with God and Christ until all is perfect and complete (the meaning of the symbolic era of "one thousand years" in Rev. 20:6).

CHAPTER IV

Concluding Observations

*I*n reviewing what has been said in the preceding pages, it will help to attempt to formulate several principles that can be observed in what the Bible says about life after death.

1. Life begins and ends with God. Life has its culmination in God, who is also the source of life. The book of Revelation expresses this idea by its affirmation that God is the *alpha* and the *omega* (the first and the last letters of the Greek alphabet), that is, the beginning and the end.

2. There is the growing hope in the biblical tradition among the faithful that they will be with God beyond death. Whereas the earlier biblical tradition assumed that humanity was present with and conversant with God only during a brief span of life (the most one could hope for was threescore and ten years, see Ps. 90:10), the growing hope was that

divine presence would be a continuing reality in the experience of humanity beyond the grave. In the development of this hope, the basic issue was the question of the justice of God. Primarily, people believed that God's justice is expressed in this life through rewards for obedience and punishment for disobedience. This deuteronomic view was dominant during much of the Old Testament period. When brave souls dared to question the traditional view and to observe that the righteous suffer and the wicked prosper (for example, Jeremiah and Job), there was an effort to find a more adequate framework for understanding the relationship between human realities and divine justice. Being unable even to consider that God is unjust, the community of faith expressed its confidence in the continuing presence of God beyond death. Since the just were not being rewarded in this life, there must be another realm in which justice will prevail.

3. Affirmations of hope for life after death are grounded in faith, in the experience of the individual and of the community of faith. Affirmations about God in this life are the basis of the affirmation of, belief in, and hope for the hereafter. If God is a God of justice, then surely justice will prevail for all eternity. The love of God, which has no limits, surely must be chronologically without end. Furthermore, the unending love that has been experienced in this life as having a personal dimension will continue to be present beyond death. For those who have experienced this boundless love of God, surely nothing can

ever separate them from God's love—not even death (see Rom. 8:35-39). Thus hope for life after death is an article of faith that cannot be proven by marshalling supportive arguments. It is an extension of the affirmation of faith in the never-ending love of God.

4. The various beliefs in life after death are expressions of the cultures from which they came. The earliest expression of belief in life after death with rewards and punishments, which appears in the book of Daniel, is developed in a cultural context that views the struggle between good and evil in terms of cosmic dualism. The book of Daniel also expresses clearly the concern for those people involved in the struggle of the Jewish community of faith, who were being persecuted because they were the people of God. Should they expire in this struggle, they will receive their reward in a realm where God dwells, the new Jerusalem, which is a projection of images from their own cultural context. For those who raise the wrath of God by persecuting the elect, the punishment will be worse than the smoldering flames of the Valley of Hinnom.

As important as understanding the spatial symbols of life after death are the views of what it means to speak of the essence of personal existence. Whether expressed in Hebraic terms, affirming the resurrection of the body, or in Greek terms, alluding to the immortality of the soul, the primary focus is on the essence of what it means to be a person. The culture shapes the particular expression of the understanding of personal existence. The belief in a continuation of personal existence is more basic than is the concern over the form of that personal existence, whatever the cultural influence.

5. The focus on continued personal existence is sometimes expressed with individual emphasis, sometimes with corporate emphasis. While there are many references to the individual, the individual seems to be ultimately connected more with communal images suggesting a community of believers. Some of these images are "the greater cloud of witnesses," "the communion of saints," "Messianic banquet," "new Jerusalem," and "the body of Christ." The primary emphasis of these images is the corporate people of God.

6. In discussing the evolution of views of life after death in the biblical traditions, it is common to affirm that if there is a change in view, then this change is associated with Jesus. Our review of the literature of the Bible does not lead to that conclusion. Rather, the development of a view of life after death emerged earlier as a solution to the problem of the justice of God. This problem arose for the Jewish people generally in the time of the exile, and there was a wrestling with the question and a search for a solution in the post-exilic period. The solution of life after death with rewards and punishments had clearly emerged by the second century B.C., as seen in the book of Daniel. This solution is further debated, developed, and refined during the intertestamental period. Jesus' affirmations about life after death and

his expression of them in apocalyptic language are, therefore, generally in continuity with the increasingly dominant view of Judaism of his day.

7. In interpreting apocalyptic literature, which is the dominant type of literature reflecting on life after death in the biblical writings, there is one basic question: Is apocalyptic literature intended as a blueprint of how history will end and of what will follow, or is it a highly symbolic affirmation of the faith that, when history does end, God will be in control and God's purpose will prevail? The latter alternative has more to commend it. While it is true that many have taken the blueprint approach and have looked for clues for the end and what lies beyond, the biblical tradition affirms that those mysteries are known only to God. Futhermore, the total character of apocalyptic literature is given to an intricate system of symbols, which encourages those who are being persecuted to persevere in the cause of right and good over the cause of wrong and evil. The overarching theme of apocalyptic literature is the ultimate triumph of God and the reward, for those who are faithful, of being in God's presence.

For anyone whose human pilgrimage has been touched by the experience of the death of one who is important, the exploration of the issue of life after death is not merely an intellectual puzzle to be solved. It is an existential reality, experienced out of the resources of one's faith. In the experience of the death of my brother, to which I alluded in the introduction, I was amazed (at least in reflective retrospection) at how suddenly and completely concerns about the form of life after death were replaced by the confidence that God would take care of him (and me!) in death as in life. Even with the overwhelming sense of loss accompanying his death, there was a confidence from within and from the supportive community of love around me (which I call the Church) that provided assurance that life would triumph over death.

This is not to say that that experience was the end of consideration of the issue of life after death as an intellectual puzzle. It was not, and may there be no end to intellectual curiosity! In my reflections, there has been an increased preoccupation with the idea that for there to be a life after death, there must be memory because without memory there is no sense of continuity that gives context to the question: Who am I?

It is this hope which is expressed on the monument at the grave of my parents:

They remain eternally a memory in the mind of God.

Bailey, Lloyd R., Sr. *Biblical Perspectives on Death* (Overtures to Biblical Theology Series). Philadelphia: Fortress Press, 1979.

Bowman, John W. "Eschatology in the NT," in *The Interpreter's Dictionary of the Bible*. Edited by George A. Buttrick et al. Vol. II, pp. 135-40. Nashville: Abingdon Press, 1962.

Charles, R. H. *Eschatology: The Doctrine of a Future Life in Israel, Judaism and Christianity*. New York: Schocken Books, 1963.

Efird, James M. *Daniel and Revelation: A Study of Two Extraordinary Visions*. Valley Forge, Penn.: Judson Press, 1978.

Eichrodt, Walther. *Theology of the Old Testament*. Vol. II. Philadelphia: Westminster Press, 1967.

Gaster, Theodor H. "Gehenna," in *The Interpreter's Dictionary of the Bible*. Edited by George A. Buttrick et al. Vol. II, pp. 361-62. Nashville: Abingdon Press, 1962.

———. "Resurrection," in *The Interpreter's Dictionary of the*

Bible. Edited by George A. Buttrick et al. Vol. IV, pp. 39-43. Nashville: Abingdon Press, 1962.

Jenni, Ernst. "Eschatology of the OT, in *The Interpreter's Dictionary of the Bible.* Edited by George A. Buttrick et al. Vol. II, pp. 126-33. Nashville: Abingdon Press, 1962.

Keck, Leander. "New Testament Views of Death," in *Perspectives on Death.* Edited by Liston O. Mills. Nashville: Abingdon Press, 1969.

Kelsey, Morton. *Afterlife: The Other Side of Dying.* New York: Paulist Press, 1979.

Knox, John. *Christ and the Hope of Glory.* New York: Abingdon, 1960.

Morris, Leon. *Apocalyptic.* Grand Rapids: Eerdmans, 1977.

Nickelsburg, George. "Future Life in Intertestamental Literature," in *The Interpreter's Dictionary of the Bible.* Edited by Keith Crim et al. Supplementary Volume, pp. 348-51. Nashville: Abingdon Press, 1976.

Page, Allen F. "Paul's Understanding of the Resurrection: An Exegesis of I Corinthians 15." M.Div. thesis, Union Theological Seminary (New York), 1964.

Rist, Martin. "Eschatology of Apocrypha and Pseudepigrapha," in *The Interpreter's Dictionary of the Bible.* Edited by George A. Buttrick et al. Vol. II, pp. 133-35. Nashville: Abingdon Press, 1962.

Robinson, J. A. T. "Resurrection in the New Testament," in *The Interpreter's Dictionary of the Bible.* Edited by George A. Buttrick et al. Vol. IV, pp. 43-57. Nashville: Abingdon Press, 1962.

Russell, David S. *The Method and Message of Jewish Apocalyptic.* The Old Testament Library. Philadelphia: Westminster Press, 1964.

Schwarz, Hans. *On the Way to the Future.* Revised edition. Minneapolis: Augsburg Publishing House, 1979.

Shires, Henry M. *The Eschatology of Paul in the Light of Modern Scholarship.* Philadelphia: Westminster Press, 1966.

Silberman, Lou H. "Death in the Hebrew Bible and Apocalyptic Literature," in *Perspectives on Death*. Edited by Liston O. Mills. Nashville: Abingdon Press, 1969.

Smith, D. Moody. *John*. Proclamation Commentaries: The New Testament Witnesses for Preaching Series. Edited by Gerhard Krodel. Philadelphia: Fortress Press, 1976.

Summers, Ray. *The Life Beyond*. Nashville: Broadman Press, 1973.